The Complete Keto Slow Cooker Cookbook

Tasty Recipes from Appetizer to Dessert With Your Crockpot Machine.
Prevent Hypertension, Heal Your Body and Boost Metabolism with Easy Guide.

Linda Walker

Table of Contents

Introduction

Slow cookers can be really useful in the kitchen and can make life so much easier. They make it so that you can prep your ingredients the day before, and they will be ready for you when you get home. The slow cooker is also great for people on a tight budget, because it can save you a lot of money in the long run. That said, it's important to know how to use your slow cooker properly. Here are some tips to help you get started.

Cook With Low Heat

Always start with low heat when cooking your ingredients in a slow cooker. If you put them over medium heat, they will burn or scorch before they are finished. Instead, start out on low heat and let them cook for several hours until they are done. This will ensure that they are safe to eat and don't have any nasty flavors left over from being cooked too fast.

Leave room at the top

Place your ingredients in the cooker as soon as possible after placing them on the stove top or in the oven. This will give them enough time to cook properly without being overcooked on high heat. If you leave them sitting in the hot pot without food inside of it, sometimes it can become stuck and won't release until you turn off the burner. This can cause some parts of your dish to be overcooked, which can ruin everything you worked so hard to perfect!

Use recipes right away

A great way to use your slow cooker is by developing some new recipes! Have fun experimenting and working on some new ones all at once without having to worry about any nasty flavors ruining your dish later on. Take note of what works well and what does not, so you end up with something delicious every time!

Slow Cookers are a great way to prepare your food and make it taste like someone else has done it for you. With the right recipe in your slow cooker, you can turn days of cooking into hours of preparation.

We've decided to share with you some of our favorite slow cooker recipes from around the country. Some recipes are classic favorites, while others are new and fresh. Whatever you're looking for, you'll find it here.

Slow cookers are a great way to prepare all kinds of meals. With the right recipe, you can cook a variety of dishes, including soups that will warm you up on a cold day.

Some of the advantages to using a slow cooker include reducing the amount of energy needed to use your electric stove. You also don't have to worry about burning yourself when using the stove. You can also leave the slow cooker on when you're not home, making it easy to prepare simple meals and snacks for your family.

You can find many recipes in our slow cooker cookbook. It's divided into several sections, including breakfast, main dishes, side dishes, desserts, and drinks. The slow cooker cookbook is designed for a number of different uses. For example, you can use it to make lots of different side dishes and desserts while you're on vacation or traveling. You can also use the same cookbook in your kitchen to prepare healthy main meals during the week or when you're having friends over for dinner.

Don't let your slow cooker get rusty with age! Contact us today to order our slow cooker cookbook at our guaranteed lowest price. We'll even ship it right away so that you can get started cooking immediately!

Tuna in Potatoes

Preparation time: 16 minutes

Cooking time: 4 hours

Servings: 8

Ingredients:

- 4 large potatoes

- 8 oz. tuna, canned

- ½ cup cream cheese

- 4 oz. Cheddar cheese

- 1 garlic clove

- 1 teaspoon onion powder

- ½ teaspoon salt

- 1 teaspoon ground black pepper

- 1 teaspoon dried dill

Directions:

1. Wash the potatoes carefully and cut them into the halves.

2. Wrap the potatoes in the foil and place in the slow cooker. Close the slow cooker lid and cook the potatoes on HIGH for 2 hours.

3. Meanwhile, peel the garlic clove and mince it. Combine the minced garlic clove with the cream cheese, tuna, salt, ground black pepper, onion powder, and dill.

4. Then shred Cheddar cheese and add it to the mixture.

5. Mix it carefully until homogenous.

6. When the time is over – remove the potatoes from the slow cooker and discard the foil only from the flat surface of the potatoes.

7. Then take the fork and mash the flesh of the potato halves gently. Add the tuna mixture in the potato halves and return them back in the slow cooker.

8. Cook the potatoes for 2 hours more on HIGH. Enjoy!

Nutrition:

Calories 247,

Fat 5.9,

Fiber 4,

Carbs 35.31,

Protein 14

Banana Lunch Sandwiches

Preparation time: 15 minutes

Cooking time: 2 hours

Servings: 4

Ingredients:

- 2 banana

- 8 oz. French toast slices, frozen

- 1 tablespoon peanut butter

- ¼ teaspoon ground cinnamon

- 5 oz. Cheddar cheese, sliced

- ¼ teaspoon turmeric

Directions:

1. Peel the bananas and slice them.

2. Spread the French toast slices with the peanut butter well. Combine the ground cinnamon with the turmeric and stir the mixture. Sprinkle the French toasts with the spice mixture.

3. Then make the layer of the sliced bananas on the toasts and add the sliced cheese.

4. Cover the toast with the second part of the toast to make the sandwich.

5. Place the banana sandwiches in the slow cooker and cook them on HIGH for 2 hours.

6. Serve the prepared banana sandwiches hot. Enjoy!

Nutrition:

Calories 248,

Fat 7.5,

Fiber 2,

Carbs 36.74,

Protein 10

Parmesan Potato with Dill

Preparation time: 17 minutes

Cooking time: 4 hours

Servings: 5

Ingredients:

- 1-pound small potato

- ½ cup fresh dill

- 7 oz. Parmesan

- 1 teaspoon rosemary

- 1 teaspoon thyme

- 1 cup water

- ¼ teaspoon chili flakes

- 3 tablespoon cream

- 1 teaspoon salt

Directions:

1. Peel the potatoes and put them in the slow cooker.

2. Add water, salt, thyme, rosemary, and chili flakes.

3. Close the slow cooker lid and cook the potato for 2 hours on HIGH.

4. Meanwhile, shred Parmesan cheese and chop the fresh dill. When the time is done, sprinkle the potato with the cream and fresh dill. Stir it carefully.

5. Add shredded Parmesan cheese and close the slow cooker lid. Cook the potato on HIGH for 2 hours more.

6. Then open the slow cooker lid and do not stir the potato anymore. Gently transfer the dish to the serving plates. Enjoy!

Nutrition:

Calories 235,

Fat 3.9,

Fiber 2,

Carbs 32.26,

Protein 1

Light Taco Soup

Preparation time: 24 minutes

Cooking time: 7 hours

Servings: 5

Ingredients:

- 7 oz. ground chicken

- ½ teaspoon sesame oil

- 3 cup vegetable stock

- 3 oz. yellow onion

- 1 cup tomato, canned

- 3 tomatoes

- 5 oz. corn kernels

- 1 jalapeno pepper, sliced

- ½ cup white beans, drained

- 3 tablespoon taco seasoning

- ¼ teaspoon salt

- 3 oz. black olives, sliced

- 5 corn tortillas, for serving

Directions:

1. Peel the onion and dice it. Chop the fresh and canned tomatoes.

2. Place the ground chicken, sesame oil, vegetable stock, diced onion, chopped tomatoes, sliced black olives, sliced jalapeno pepper, and corn in the slow cooker.

3. Add the white beans, taco seasoning, and salt.

4. Stir the soup mixture gently and close the slow cooker lid.

5. Cook the soup for 7 hours on LOW. Meanwhile, cut the corn tortillas into the strips and bake them in the preheated to 365 F oven for 10 minutes.

6. When the soup is cooked, ladle it into the serving bowls and sprinkle with the baked corn tortilla strips. Enjoy!

Nutrition:

Calories 328,

Fat 9.6,

Fiber 10,

Carbs 45.19,

Protein 18

Slow Cooker Risotto

Preparation time: 20 minutes

Cooking time: 3 hours 30 minutes

Servings: 6

Ingredients:

- 7 oz. Parmigiano-Reggiano

- 2 cup chicken broth

- 1 teaspoon olive oil

- 1 onion, chopped

- ½ cup green peas

- 1 garlic clove, peeled and sliced

- 2 cups long grain rice

- ¼ cup dry wine

- 1 teaspoon salt

- 1 teaspoon ground black pepper

- 1 carrot, chopped

- 1 cup beef broth

Directions:

1. Spray a skillet with olive oil.

2. Add the chopped onion and carrot and roast the vegetables for 3 minutes on the medium heat. Then put the seared vegetables in the slow cooker. Toss the long grain rice in the remaining oil and sauté for 1 minute on the high heat.

3. Add the roasted long grain rice and sliced garlic in the slow cooker.

4. Add green peas, dry wine, salt, ground black pepper, and beef broth. After this, add the chicken broth and stir the mixture gently. Close the slow cooker lid and cook the risotto for 3 hours.

5. Then stir the risotto gently.

6. Shred Parmigiano-Reggiano and sprinkle over the risotto. Close the slow cooker lid and cook the dish

for 30 minutes more. Enjoy the prepared risotto immediately!

Nutrition:

Calories 268,

Fat 3,

Fiber 4,

Carbs 53.34,

Protein 7

Lemon Orzo

Preparation time: 20 minutes

Cooking time: 2 hours 30 minutes

Servings: 5

Ingredients:

- 4 oz. shallot

- 7 oz. orzo

- 2 cup chicken stock

- 1 teaspoon paprika

- 1 teaspoon ground black pepper

- 1 teaspoon salt

- 1 lemon

- ¼ cup cream

- 2 yellow sweet pepper

- 1 cup baby spinach

Directions:

1. Chop the shallot and place it in the slow cooker.

2. Add the chicken stock and paprika. Sprinkle the mixture with the ground black pepper and salt. Stir it gently and cook on HIGH for 30 minutes.

3. Meanwhile, grate the zest from the lemon and squeeze the juice. Add the lemon zest and juice in the slow cooker and stir it. After this, chop the baby spinach.

4. Add it into the slow cooker. Remove the seeds from the yellow sweet peppers and chop into tiny pieces. Add the chopped peppers to the slow cooker.

5. Add orzo and heavy cream. Stir the mass carefully and close the slow cooker lid. Cook the dish for 2 hours on LOW. Mix the dish gently. Enjoy!

Nutrition:

Calories 152,

Fat 4,

Fiber 3,

Carbs 24.79,

Protein 7

Veggie Bean Stew

Preparation time: 20 minutes

Cooking time: 7 hours

Servings: 8

Ingredients:

- ½ cup barley

- 1 cup black beans

- ¼ cup red beans

- 2 carrots

- 1 cup onion, chopped

- 1 cup tomato juice

- 2 potatoes

- 1 teaspoon salt

- 1 teaspoon ground black pepper

- 4 cups water

- 4 oz. tofu

- 1 teaspoon garlic powder

- 1 cup fresh cilantro

Directions:

1. Place barley, black beans, and red beans in the slow cooker vessel.

2. Add chopped onion, tomato juice, salt, ground black pepper, and garlic powder. After this, add water and close the slow cooker lid.

3. Cook the dish for 4 hours on HIGH.

4. Meanwhile, peel the carrots and cut them into the strips. Peel the potatoes and chop.

5. Add the carrot strips and chopped potatoes in the slow cooker after 4 hours of cooking.

6. Chop the fresh cilantro and add it in the slow cooker too.

7. Stir the mix and close the slow cooker lid. Cook the stew for 3 hours more on LOW.

8. Serve the prepared dish immediately or keep it in the fridge, not more than 3 days. Enjoy!

Nutrition:

Calories 207,

Fat 3.5,

Fiber 8,

Carbs 37.67,

Protein 8

Carrot Soup with Cardamom

Preparation time: 18 minutes

Cooking time: 12 hours

Servings: 9

Ingredients:

- 1-pound carrot

- 1 teaspoon ground cardamom

- ¼ teaspoon nutmeg

- 1 teaspoon salt

- 3 tablespoons fresh parsley

- 1 teaspoon honey

- 1 teaspoon marjoram

- 5 cups chicken stock

- ½ cup yellow onion, chopped

- 1 teaspoon butter

Directions:

1. Toss the butter in a pan and add chopped onion.

2. Chop the carrot and add it to the pan too.

3. Roast the vegetables for 5 minutes on the low heat. After this, place the roasted vegetables in the slow cooker. Add ground cardamom, nutmeg, salt, marjoram, and chicken stock.

4. Close the slow cooker lid and cook the soup for 12 hours on LOW.

5. Chop the fresh parsley.

6. When the time is over, blend the soup with a hand blender until you get a smooth texture. Then ladle the soup into the serving bowls.

7. Sprinkle the prepared soup with the chopped fresh parsley and honey. Enjoy the soup immediately!

Nutrition:

Calories 80,

Fat 2.7,

Fiber 2,

Carbs 10.19,

Protein 4

Cod Chowder

Preparation time: 20 minutes

Cooking time: 3 hours

Servings: 6

Ingredients:

- 1 yellow onion

- 10 oz. cod

- 3 oz. bacon, sliced

- 1 teaspoon sage

- 5 oz. potatoes

- 1 carrot, grated

- 5 cups water

- 1 tablespoon almond milk

- 1 teaspoon ground coriander

- 1 teaspoon salt

Directions:

1. Peel the onion and chop it.

2. Put the chopped onion and grated carrot in the slow cooker bowl. Add the sage, almond milk, ground coriander, and water. After this, chop the cod into the 6 pieces.

3. Add the fish in the slow cooker bowl too. Then chop the sliced bacon and peel the potatoes.

4. Cut the potatoes into the cubes.

5. Add the Ingredients in the slow cooker bowl and close the slow cooker lid.

6. Cook the chowder for 3 hours on HIGH. Ladle the prepared cod chowder in the serving bowls.

7. Sprinkle the dish with the chopped parsley if desired. Enjoy!

Nutrition:

Calories 108,

Fat 4.5,

Fiber 2,

Carbs 8.02,

Protein 10

Lunch Chicken Wraps

Preparation time: 18 minutes

Cooking time: 6 hours

Servings: 6

Ingredients:

- 6 tortillas

- 3 tablespoon Caesar dressing

- 1-pound chicken breast

- ½ cup lettuce

- 1 cup water

- 1 oz. bay leaf

- 1 teaspoon salt

- 1 teaspoon ground pepper

- 1 teaspoon coriander

- 4 oz. Feta cheese

Directions:

1. Put the chicken breast in the slow cooker.

2. Sprinkle the meat with the bay leaf, salt, ground pepper, and coriander.

3. Add water and cook the chicken breast for 6 hours on LOW.

4. Then remove the cooked chicken from the slow cooker and shred it with a fork.

5. Chop the lettuce roughly.

6. Then chop Feta cheese. Combine the chopped **Ingredients:** together and add the shredded chicken breast and Caesar dressing.

7. Mix everything together well. After this, spread the tortillas with the shredded chicken mixture and wrap them. Enjoy!

Nutrition:

Calories 376,

Fat 18.5,

Fiber 3,

Carbs 29.43,

Protein 23

Nutritious Lunch Wraps

Preparation time: 20 minutes

Cooking time: 4 hours

Servings: 5

Ingredients:

- 7 oz. ground pork

- 5 tortillas

- 1 tablespoon tomato paste

- ½ cup onion, chopped

- ½ cup lettuce

- 1 teaspoon ground black pepper

- 1 teaspoon salt

- 1 teaspoon sour cream

- 5 tablespoons water

- 4 oz. Parmesan, shredded

- 2 tomatoes

Directions:

1. Combine the ground pork with the tomato paste, ground black pepper, salt, and sour cream. Transfer the meat mixture to the slow cooker and cook on HIGH for 4 hours.

2. Meanwhile, chop the lettuce roughly. Slice the tomatoes.

3. Place the sliced tomatoes in the tortillas and add the chopped lettuce and shredded Parmesan. When the ground pork is cooked, chill to room temperature.

4. Add the ground pork in the tortillas and wrap them. Enjoy!

Nutrition:

Calories 318,

Fat 7,

Fiber 2,

Carbs 3.76,

Protein 26

Butternut Squash Soup

Preparation time: 10 minutes

Cooking time: 8 hours

Servings: 9

Ingredients:

- 2-pound butternut squash

- 4 teaspoon minced garlic

- ½ cup onion, chopped

- 1 teaspoon salt

- ¼ teaspoon ground nutmeg

- 1 teaspoon ground black pepper

- 8 cups chicken stock

- 1 tablespoon fresh parsley

Directions:

1. Peel the butternut squash and cut it into the chunks.

2. Toss the butternut squash in the slow cooker.

3. Add chopped onion, minced garlic, and chicken stock.

4. Close the slow cooker lid and cook the soup for 8 hours on LOW.

5. Meanwhile, combine the ground black pepper, ground nutmeg, and salt together.

6. Chop the fresh parsley.

7. When the time is done, remove the soup from the slow cooker and blend it with a blender until you get a creamy soup.

8. Sprinkle the soup with the spice mixture and add chopped parsley. Serve the soup warm. Enjoy!

Nutrition:

Calories 129,

Fat 2.7,

Fiber 2,

Carbs 20.85,

Protein 7

Eggplant Bacon Wraps

Preparation time: 17 minutes

Cooking time: 5 hours

Servings: 6

Ingredients:

- 10 oz. eggplant, sliced into rounds

- 5 oz. halloumi cheese

- 1 teaspoon minced garlic

- 3 oz. bacon, chopped

- ½ teaspoon ground black pepper

- 1 teaspoon salt

- 1 teaspoon paprika

- 1 tomato

Directions:

1. Rub the eggplant slices with the ground black pepper, salt, and paprika.

2. Slice halloumi cheese and tomato.

3. Combine the chopped bacon and minced garlic together.

4. Place the sliced eggplants in the slow cooker. Cook the eggplant on HIGH for 1 hour.

5. Chill the eggplant. Place the sliced tomato and cheese on the eggplant slices.

6. Add the chopped bacon mixture and roll up tightly.

7. Secure the eggplants with the toothpicks and return the eggplant wraps back into the slow cooker. Cook the dish on HIGH for 4 hours more.

8. When the dish is done, serve it immediately. Enjoy!

Nutrition:

Calories 131,

Fat 9.4,

Fiber 2,

Carbs 7.25,

Protein 6

Mexican Warm Salad

Preparation time: 26 minutes

Cooking time: 10 hours

Servings: 10

Ingredients:

- 1 cup black beans

- 1 cup sweet corn, frozen

- 3 tomatoes

- ½ cup fresh dill

- 1 chili pepper

- 7 oz. chicken fillet

- 5 oz. Cheddar cheese

- 4 tablespoons mayonnaise

- 1 teaspoon minced garlic

- 1 cup lettuce

- 5 cups chicken stock

- 1 cucumber

Directions:

1. Put the chicken fillet, sweet corn, black beans, and chicken stock in the slow cooker.

2. Close the slow cooker lid and cook the mixture on LOW for 10 hours.

3. When the time is done remove the mixture from the slow cooker.

4. Shred the chicken fillet with 2 forks. Chill the mixture until room temperature.

5. Chop the lettuce roughly. Chop the cucumber and tomatoes.

6. Place the lettuce, cucumber, and tomatoes on a large serving plate.

7. After this, shred Cheddar cheese and chop the chili pepper.

8. Add the chili pepper to the serving plate too.

9. After this, add the chicken mixture on the top of the salad.

10. Sprinkle the salad with the mayonnaise, minced garlic, and shredded cheese. Enjoy the salad immediately.

Nutrition:

Calories 182,

Fat 7.8,

Fiber 2,

Carbs 19.6,

Stuffed Eggplants

Preparation time: 20 minutes

Cooking time: 8 hours

Servings: 4

Ingredients:

- 4 medium eggplants

- 1 cup rice, half cooked

- ½ cup chicken stock

- 1 teaspoon salt

- 1 teaspoon paprika

- ½ cup fresh cilantro

- 3 tablespoons tomato sauce

- 1 teaspoon olive oil

Directions:

1. Wash the eggplants carefully and remove the flesh from them.

2. Then combine the rice with the salt, paprika, and tomato sauce.

3. Chop the fresh cilantro and add it to the rice mixture.

4. Then fill the prepared eggplants with the rice mixture.

5. Pour the chicken stock and olive oil in the slow cooker.

6. Add the stuffed eggplants and close the slow cooker lid.

7. Cook the dish on LOW for 8 hours. When the eggplants are done, chill them little and serve immediately. Enjoy!

Nutrition:

Calories 277,

Fat 9.1,

Fiber 24,

Carbs 51.92,

Protein 11

Light Lunch Quiche

Preparation time: 21 minutes

Cooking time: 4 hours 25 minutes

Servings: 7

Ingredients:

- 7 oz. pie crust

- ¼ cup broccoli

- 1/3 cup sweet peas

- ¼ cup heavy cream

- 2 tablespoons flour

- 3 eggs

- 4 oz. Romano cheese, shredded

- 1 teaspoon cilantro

- 1 teaspoon salt

- ¼ cup spinach

- 1 tomato

Directions:

1. Cover the inside of the slow cooker bowl with parchment.

2. Put the pie crust inside and flatten it well with your fingertips.

3. Chop the broccoli and combine it with sweet peas. Combine the heavy cream, flour, cilantro, and salt together. Stir the liquid until smooth.

4. Then beat the eggs into the heavy cream liquid and mix it with a hand mixer. When you get a smooth mix, combine it with the broccoli.

5. Chop the spinach and add it to the mix. Chop the tomato and add it to the mix too. Pour the prepared mixture into the pie crust slowly.

6. Close the slow cooker lid and cook the quiche for 4 hours on HIGH.

7. After 4 hours, sprinkle the quiche surface with the shredded cheese and cook the dish for 25 minutes more. Serve the prepared quiche! Enjoy!

Nutrition:

Calories 287,

Fat 18.8,

Fiber 1,

Carbs 17.1,

Protein 11

Chicken Open Sandwich

Preparation time: 15 minutes

Cooking time: 8 hours

Servings: 4

Ingredients:

- 7 oz. chicken fillet

- 1 teaspoon cayenne pepper

- 5 oz. mashed potato, cooked

- 6 tablespoons chicken gravy

- 4 slices French bread, toasted

- 2 teaspoons mayo

- 1 cup water

Directions:

1. Put the chicken fillet in the slow cooker and sprinkle it with the cayenne pepper.

2. Add water and chicken gravy. Close the slow cooker lid and cook the chicken for 8 hours on LOW. Then combine the mashed potato with the mayo sauce.

3. Spread toasted French bread with the mashed potato mixture.

4. When the chicken is cooked, cut it into the strips and combine with the remaining gravy from the slow cooker.

5. Place the chicken strips over the mashed potato. Enjoy the open sandwich warm!

Nutrition:

Calories 314,

Fat 9.7,

Fiber 3,

Carbs 45.01,

Protein 12

Onion Lunch Muffins

Preparation time: 15 minutes
Cooking time: 8 hours
Servings: 7
Ingredients:

- 1 egg

- 5 tablespoons butter, melted

- 1 cup flour

- ½ cup milk

- 1 teaspoon baking soda

- 1 cup onion, chopped

- 1 teaspoon cilantro

- ½ teaspoon sage

- 1 teaspoon apple cider vinegar

- 2 cup water

- 1 tablespoon chives

- 1 teaspoon olive oil

Directions:

1. Beat the egg in the bowl and add melted butter.

---

2. Add the flour, baking soda, chopped onion, milk, sage, apple cider vinegar, cilantro, and chives. Knead into a dough.

3. After this, spray a muffin form with the olive oil inside. Fill the ½ part of every muffin form and place them in the glass jars.

4. After this, pour water in the slow cooker vessel.

5. Place the glass jars with muffins in the slow cooker and close the lid.

6. Cook the muffins for 8 hours on LOW.

7. Check if the muffins are cooked with the help of the toothpick and remove them from the slow cooker. Enjoy the dish warm!

Nutrition:

Calories 180,

Fat 11,

Fiber 1,

Carbs 16.28,

Protein 4

Garlic Duck Breast

Preparation time: 20 minutes

Cooking time: 5 hours

Servings: 6

Ingredients:

- 11 oz. duck breast, boneless, skinless

- 4 garlic cloves, roughly diced

- 1 teaspoon rosemary

- 1 tablespoon butter

- ½ cup water

- 1 teaspoon chili flakes

Directions:

1. Make small cuts in the duck breast.

2. Sprinkle the duck breast with the rosemary and chili flakes.

3. Fill the cuts with the diced garlic.

4. Place the duck breast in the slow cooker.

5. Add butter and water and close the lid.

6. Cook the duck breast for 5 hours on Low.

7. When the duck breast is cooked, remove it from the slow cooker and let it rest for 10 minutes.

8. Slice the duck breast and serve!

Nutrition:

Calories 268,

Fat 3,

Fiber 4,

Carbs 53.34,

Protein 7

Thyme Lamb Chops

Preparation time: 20 minutes

Cooking time: 7 hours

Servings: 2

Ingredients:

- 8 oz. lamb chops

- 1 teaspoon liquid stevia

- 1 teaspoon thyme

- 1 tablespoon olive oil

- ¼ cup water

- 1 bay leaf

- ¾ teaspoon ground cinnamon

- ½ onion, chopped

Directions:

1. Mix the liquid stevia, thyme, olive oil, and ground cinnamon.

2. Rub the lamb chops with the spice mixture.

3. Place the lamb chops in the slow cooker and add chopped onion and water.

4. Add the bay leaf and close the lid.

5. Cook the lamb chops for 7 hours on Low.

6. When the meat is cooked, serve it immediately!

Nutrition:

Calories 368,

Fat 3,

Fiber 4,

Carbs 53.34,

Protein 7

Autumn Pork Stew

Preparation time: 30 minutes

Cooking time: 6 hours

Servings: 5

Ingredients:

- 1 eggplant, chopped

- 4 oz. white mushrooms, chopped

- 1 white onion, chopped

- 2 cups water

- ½ teaspoon clove

- ½ teaspoon salt

- ½ teaspoon cayenne pepper

- 8 oz. pork tenderloin

Directions:

1. Place the chopped eggplant, mushrooms, onion, and water in the slow cooker.

2. Chop the pork tenderloin roughly and sprinkle it with the cayenne pepper, salt, and clove.

3. Stir the meat and place it in the slow cooker too.

4. Close the lid and cook the stew for 6 hours on Low.

5. When the stew is cooked, let it rest for 20 minutes.

6. Enjoy!

Nutrition:

Calories 168,

Fat 3,

Fiber 4,

Carbs 53.34,

Protein 7

Handmade Sausage Stew

Preparation time: 25 minutes

Cooking time: 3 hours

Servings: 3

Ingredients:

- 7 oz. ground pork

- 1 egg yolk

- ½ teaspoon salt

- ½ teaspoon ground black pepper

- 7 oz. broccoli, chopped

- ½ cup water

- 1 tomato, chopped

- 1 teaspoon butter

Directions:

1. Mix the ground pork and yolk. Add salt and ground black pepper.

2. Stir the mixture and form small sausages with your hands.

3. Place the sausages in the slow cooker.

4. Add the chopped broccoli and water.

5. Add chopped tomato and butter.

6. Close the lid and cook the stew for 3 hours on High.

7. Place the cooked stew in bowls and enjoy!

Nutrition:

Calories 268,

Fat 3,

Fiber 4,

Carbs 53.34,

Protein 7

Marinated Beef Tenderloin

Preparation time: 20 minutes

Cooking time: 6 hours

Servings: 6

Ingredients:

- 2 tablespoons butter

- 1-pound Beef Tenderloin

- 1 teaspoon minced garlic

- ½ teaspoon ground nutmeg

- 1 teaspoon turmeric

- 1 teaspoon paprika

- 1 tablespoon apple cider vinegar

- ½ teaspoon dried oregano

- 1 cup water

Directions:

1. Melt the butter and mix it up with the minced garlic, ground nutmeg, turmeric, paprika, apple cider vinegar, and dried oregano.

2. Whisk the mixture.

3. Rub the beef tenderloin with the spice mixture.

4. Place the beef tenderloin in the slow cooker and add the remaining spice mixture.

5. Add water and close the lid.

6. Cook the beef tenderloin for 8 hours on Low.

7. Chop the beef tenderloin and serve it!

Nutrition:

Calories 68,

Fat 3,

Fiber 4,

Carbs 53.34,

Protein 7

Chicken Liver Sauté

Preparation time: 20 minutes

Cooking time: 5 hours

Servings: 4

Ingredients:

- 10 oz. chicken liver

- 1 onion, chopped

- 2 tablespoons full-fat cream

- 5 oz. white mushrooms, chopped

- 1 cup water

- 1 tablespoon butter

- 1 teaspoon salt

- ½ teaspoon ground black pepper

Directions:

1. Place the chicken liver, onion, full-fat cream, mushrooms, water, butter, salt, and ground black pepper in the slow cooker and close the lid.

2. Cook the mixture for 5 hours on Low.

3. When the liver saute is cooked, let it rest for 10 minutes.

4. Enjoy!

Nutrition:

Calories 168,

Fat 3,

Fiber 4,

Carbs 53.34,

Protein 7

Chicken in Bacon

Preparation time: 20 minutes

Cooking time: 3 hours

Servings: 6

Ingredients:

- 1-pound chicken thighs

- 7 oz. bacon, sliced

- 1 tablespoon butter

- ¾ cup water

- ½ teaspoon ground black pepper

- 1 teaspoon chili flakes

- 1 teaspoon paprika

Directions:

1. Sprinkle the chicken thighs with the ground black pepper, chili flakes, and paprika.

2. Wrap the chicken thighs in the sliced bacon and transfer to the slow cooker.

3. Add the water and butter and close the lid.

4. Cook the chicken for 3 hours on High.

5. Serve the cooked meal immediately!

Nutrition:

Calories 268,

Fat 3,

Fiber 4,

Carbs 53.34,

Protein 7

Whole Chicken

Preparation time: 40 minutes

Cooking time: 10 hours

Servings: 10

Ingredients:

- 2-pound whole chicken

- 4 oz. celery stalk, chopped

- 1 onion, chopped

- 3 garlic cloves, peeled

- 1 tablespoon rosemary

- 1 teaspoon dried oregano

- 2 tablespoons butter

- 1 teaspoon salt

- ½ teaspoon ground coriander

- 1 teaspoon turmeric

- 2 cups water

Directions:

1. Rub the chicken with the rosemary, dried oregano, salt, ground coriander, and turmeric.

2. Fill the chicken cavity with the chopped celery, garlic cloves, onion, and butter.

3. Place the chicken in the slow cooker and add water.

4. Close the lid and cook the chicken for 10 hours on Low.

5. When the chicken is cooked, leave it for 20 minutes to rest.

6. Serve and enjoy!

Nutrition:

Calories 248,

Fat 7.5,

Fiber 2,

Carbs 36.74,

Protein 10

Duck Rolls

Preparation time: 25 minutes

Cooking time: 3 hours

Servings: 6

Ingredients:

- 2-pound duck fillets

- 1 teaspoon minced garlic

- 1 cup spinach, chopped

- ¼ cup water

- 1 teaspoon rosemary

- 1 tablespoon olive oil

Directions:

1. Beat the duck fillets gently to tenderize and flatten then sprinkle them with the minced garlic, rosemary, and olive oil.

2. Place the chopped spinach on each of the duck fillets and roll them up, enclosing the spinach inside the duck.

3. Secure the duck rolls with the toothpicks and place them in the slow cooker.

4. Add water and close the lid.

5. Cook the duck rolls for 3 hours on High.

6. Cool the rolls slightly and serve!

Nutrition:

Calories 248,

Fat 7.5,

Fiber 2,

Carbs 36.74,

Protein 10

Keto Adobo Chicken

Preparation time: 15 minutes

Cooking time: 2 hours

Servings: 4

Ingredients:

- 1-pound chicken breast, boneless, skinless

- 1 tablespoon soy sauce

- 1 tablespoon olive oil

- 1 tablespoon apple cider vinegar

- 1 teaspoon minced garlic

Directions:

1. Chop the chicken breast roughly and sprinkle it with the soy sauce, olive oil, apple cider vinegar, and minced garlic.

2. Mix and then let sit for 20 minutes to marinate.

3. Transfer the chicken and all the remaining liquid into the slow cooker.

4. Close the lid and cook the meal for 2 hours on High.

5. Enjoy!

Nutrition:

Calories 348,

Fat 7.5,

Fiber 2,

Carbs 36.74,

Protein 10

Cayenne Pepper Drumsticks

Preparation time: 20 minutes

Cooking time: 5 hours

Servings: 2

Ingredients:

- 10 oz. chicken drumsticks

- 1 teaspoon cayenne pepper

- 1 bell pepper, chopped

- ½ cup water

- 1 tablespoon butter

- 1 teaspoon thyme

- 1 teaspoon cumin

- ½ teaspoon chili pepper

Directions:

1. Mix the cayenne pepper, chopped bell pepper, butter, thyme, cumin, and chili pepper.

2. Stir the mixture until smooth,

3. Rub the chicken drumsticks with the spice mixture and place them in the slow cooker.

4. Add water and close the lid.

5. Cook the drumsticks for 5 hours on Low.

6. Transfer the cooked meal onto a platter and serve!

Nutrition:

Calories 248,

Fat 7.5,

Fiber 2,

Carbs 36.74,

Protein 10

Keto BBQ Chicken Wings

Preparation time: 20 minutes

Cooking time: 2 hours

Servings: 4

Ingredients:

- 1-pound chicken wings

- 1 teaspoon minced garlic

- 1 teaspoon cumin

- 1 teaspoon ground coriander

- 1 teaspoon dried dill

- 1 teaspoon dried parsley

- 1 tablespoon mustard

- 1 teaspoon liquid stevia

- 1 tablespoon tomato paste

- 1 teaspoon salt

- 1 tablespoon apple cider vinegar

Directions:

1. Mix the minced garlic, cumin, ground coriander, dried dill, dried parsley, mustard, liquid stevia, tomato paste, salt, and apple cider vinegar.

2. Stir the mixture until smooth.

3. Combine the spice mixture and chicken wings and stir well.

4. Transfer the chicken wings and all the remaining spice mixture into the slow cooker.

5. Close the lid and cook for 2 hours on High.

6. Cool the chicken wings slightly and serve!

Nutrition:

Calories 148,

Fat 7.5,

Fiber 2,

Carbs 36.74,

Protein 10

Sweet Corn Pilaf

Preparation time: 21 minutes

Cooking time: 8 hours

Servings: 5

Ingredients:

- 2 cups rice

- 1 cup sweet corn, frozen

- 6 oz. chicken fillet

- 1 sweet red pepper

- 1 yellow sweet pepper

- ½ cup green peas, frozen

- 1 carrot

- 4 cups chicken stock

- 2 tablespoon chopped almonds

- 1 teaspoon olive oil

- 1 teaspoon salt

- 1 teaspoon ground white pepper

Directions:

1. Peel the carrot and cut into the small cubes.

2. Combine the carrot cubes with the frozen sweet corn and green peas.

3. After this, place the vegetable mixture in the slow cooker vessel.

4. Add the rice, chicken stock, olive oil, salt, and ground white pepper.

5. After this, cut the chicken fillet into the strips and add the meat to the rice mixture.

6. Chop all the sweet peppers and add them in the slow cooker too.

7. Close the slow cooker lid and cook the pilaf for 8 hours on LOW.

8. When the pilaf is cooked, stir it gently and sprinkle with the almonds. Mix the dish carefully again. Serve it immediately. Enjoy!

Nutrition:

Calories 390,

Fat 18.6,

Fiber 13,

Carbs 54.7,

Protein 18

Mediterranean Vegetable Mix

Preparation time: 15 minutes

Cooking time: 7 hours

Servings: 8

Ingredients:

- 1 zucchini

- 2 eggplants

- 2 red onion

- 4 potatoes

- 4 oz. asparagus

- 2 tablespoon olive oil

- 1 teaspoon ground black pepper

- 1 teaspoon paprika

- 1 teaspoon salt

- 1 tablespoon Mediterranean seasoning

- 1 teaspoon minced garlic

Directions:

1. Combine the olive oil, Mediterranean seasoning, salt, paprika, ground black pepper, and minced garlic together.

2. Whisk the mixture well. Wash all the vegetables carefully.

3. Cut the zucchini, eggplants, and potatoes into the medium cubes. Cut the asparagus into 2 parts.

4. Then peel the onions and cut them into 4 parts. Toss all the vegetables in the slow cooker and sprinkle them with the spice mixture.

5. Close the slow cooker lid and cook the vegetable mix for 7 hours on LOW.

6. Serve the prepared vegetable mix hot. Enjoy!

Nutrition:

Calories 227,

Fat 3.9,

Fiber 9,

Carbs 44.88,

Protein 6

Spaghetti Cottage Cheese Casserole

Preparation time: 21 minutes

Cooking time: 7 hours

Servings: 8

Ingredients:

- 1-pound cottage cheese

- 7 oz. spaghetti, cooked

- 5 eggs

- 1 cup heavy cream

- 5 tablespoons semolina

- 3 tablespoons white sugar

- 1 teaspoon vanilla extract

- 1 teaspoon marjoram

- 1 teaspoon lemon zest

- 1 teaspoon butter

Directions:

1. Blend the cottage cheese in the blender for 1 minute to fluff.

2. Beat the eggs in the cottage mixture and continue to blend it for 3 minutes more on medium speed. Add the heavy cream, semolina, white sugar, vanilla

---

extract, marjoram, lemon zest, and butter. Blend the mixture on the maximum speed for 1 minute.

3. Then chopped the cooked spaghetti. Place 3 tablespoon of the cottage cheese mixture in the slow cooker to make the bottom layer.

4. After this, make a layer from the chopped cooked spaghetti.

5. Repeat the steps till you use all the chopped spaghetti.

6. Then spread the last layer of the spaghetti with the cottage cheese mixture and close the slow cooker lid. Cook the casserole for 7 hours on LOW.

7. When the casserole is cooked, it will have a light brown color. Serve it warm and enjoy!

Nutrition:

Calories: 302g,

Fat: 22g,

Carbs: 5g,

Protein: 34g,

Meatballs with Coconut Gravy

Preparation time: 20 minutes

Cooking time: 7 hours

Servings: 8

Ingredients:

- 3 tablespoons coconut

- 1 tablespoon curry paste

- 1 teaspoon salt

- 1 cup heavy cream

- 1 tablespoon flour

- 1 teaspoon cayenne pepper

- 10 oz. ground pork

- 1 egg

- 1 tablespoon semolina

- ½ cup onion, chopped

- 1 teaspoon kosher salt

- 3 tablespoons bread crumbs

- 1 teaspoon ground black pepper

Directions:

1. Combine the coconut, curry paste, and salt together.

2. Add heavy cream and flour.

3. Whisk the mixture and pour in the slow cooker. Cook on the LOW for 1 hour.

4. Meanwhile, beat the egg in the big bowl and whisk.

5. Add the cayenne pepper, ground pork, semolina, chopped onion, kosher salt, bread crumbs, and ground black pepper. Mix well and then make the small balls from the meat mixture and place them in the slow cooker.

6. Coat the meatballs with the prepared coconut gravy and close the lid.

7. Cook the dish for 7 hours on LOW. When the meatballs are cooked, serve them only with the coconut gravy. Enjoy!

Nutrition:

Calories: 312g,

Fat: 22g,

Carbs: 5g,

Protein: 34g,

Fresh Dal

Preparation time: 15 minutes

Cooking time: 5 hours

Servings: 11

Ingredients:

- 1 teaspoon cumin

- 1 oz. mustard seeds

- 10 oz. lentils

- 1 teaspoon fennel seeds

- 7 cups water

- 6 oz. tomato, canned

- 4 oz. onion

- ½ teaspoon fresh ginger, grated

- 1 oz. bay leaf

- 1 teaspoon turmeric

- 1 teaspoon salt

- 2 cups rice

Directions:

1. Peel the onion. Chop the onion and tomatoes and place them in a slow cooker.

2. Combine the cumin, mustard seeds, and fennel seeds in a shallow bowl.

3. Add the bay leaf and mix. Sprinkle the vegetables in the slow cooker with the spice mixture.

4. Add salt, turmeric, and grated fresh ginger. Add rice and mix.

5. Add the lentils and water. Stir gently.

6. Then close the slow cooker lid and cook Dal for 5 hours on LOW.

7. When the dish is done, stir and transfer to serving plates. Enjoy!

Nutrition:

Calories: 102g,

Fat: 22g,

Carbs: 5g,

Protein: 34g,

Pulled Pork Salad

Preparation time: 15 minutes

Cooking time: 8 hours

Servings: 4

Ingredients:

- 1 avocado, chopped

- 1 tomato, chopped

- 1 cup lettuce, chopped

- 1 tablespoon olive oil

- ½ teaspoon chili flakes

- 7 oz. pork loin

- 1 cup water

- 1 bay leaf

- 1 teaspoon salt

- ¼ teaspoon peppercorns

Directions:

1. Place the pork loin in the slow cooker.

2. Add the water, bay leaf, salt, and peppercorns.

3. Add the chili flakes and close the lid.

4. Cook the pork loin for 8 hours on Low.

5. Meanwhile, mix the chopped avocado, tomato, and lettuce in a large salad bowl.

6. When the pork loin is cooked, remove it from the water and place it in a separate bowl.

7. Shred the pork loin with two forks.

8. Add the shredded pork loin into the salad bowl.

9. Stir the salad gently and sprinkle with the olive oil.

10. Enjoy!

Nutrition:

Calories: 302g,

Fat: 22g,

Carbs: 5g,

Protein: 34g,

Garlic Pork Belly

Preparation time: 15 minutes

Cooking time: 7 hours

Servings: 8

Ingredients:

- 1-pound pork belly

- 4 garlic cloves, peeled

- 1 teaspoon peppercorns

- 2 tablespoons mustard

- ½ teaspoon salt

- 1 tablespoon butter

- 1 cup water

Directions:

1. Dice the garlic cloves and combine them with the peppercorns and mustard.

2. Add the salt and butter and stir.

3. Rub the pork belly with the prepared mixture well.

4. Place the pork belly in the slow cooker.

5. Add the water and close the lid.

6. Cook the pork belly for 7 hours on Low.

7. Slice the cooked pork belly and serve!

Nutrition:

Calories: 321g,

Fat: 22g,

Carbs: 5g,

Protein: 34g,

Sesame Seed Shrimp

Preparation time: 20 minutes

Cooking time: 30 minutes

Servings: 4

Ingredients:

- 1-pound shrimp, peeled

- 2 tablespoons apple cider vinegar

- 1 teaspoon paprika

- 1 teaspoon sesame seeds

- ¼ cup water

- 3 tablespoons butter

Directions:

1. Sprinkle the shrimp with the apple cider vinegar.

2. Add paprika and stir the shrimp.

3. Let the shrimp marinade for 15 minutes.

4. Pour water into the slow cooker.

5. Add the butter and marinated shrimp.

6. Cook the shrimp for 30 minutes on High.

7. Transfer the shrimp to a serving bowl.

8. Mix together the remaining liquid and sesame seeds.

9. Sprinkle the shrimp with the sesame mixture and enjoy!

Nutrition:

Calories: 102g,

Fat: 22g,

Carbs: 5g,

Protein: 34g,

Cod Fillet in Coconut Flakes

Preparation time: 20 minutes

Cooking time: 1 hour

Servings: 4

Ingredients:

- ¼ cup coconut flakes, unsweetened

- 1 egg, beaten

- ½ teaspoon salt

- 1 teaspoon ground black pepper

- 10 oz. cod fillets

- 1 tablespoon butter

- 3 tablespoons water

Directions:

1. Whisk the egg, combine it with the salt, and ground black pepper.

2. Place the cod fillets in the egg mixture and stir well.

3. Coat the egged cod fillets in the coconut flakes.

4. Add the butter to the slow cooker.

5. Add water and coated cod fillets.

6. Close the lid and cook the fish for 1 hour on High.

7. Then transfer the cod fillets onto a cutting board and cut them into servings.

8. Enjoy the cod fillet warm!

Nutrition:

Calories 268,

Fat 3,

Fiber 4,

Carbs 53.34,

Protein 7

Chicken Liver Pate

Preparation time: 25 minutes

Cooking time: 2 hours

Servings: 6

Ingredients:

- 1-pound chicken liver

- 1 onion, chopped

- 2 cups water

- 1 teaspoon salt

- ¼ teaspoon ground nutmeg

- 2 tablespoons butter

- 1 bay leaf

Directions:

1. Place the chicken liver in the slow cooker.

2. Add chopped onion, water, salt, ground black pepper, and bay leaf.

3. Close the lid and cook the liver for 2 hours on High.

4. After this, strain the chicken liver, discarding the liquid, and place it in the blender.

5. Add butter and blend the mixture until smooth (approximately for 3 minutes at maximum speed).

6. Transfer the cooked pate into a bowl and let it cool in the freezer for 10 minutes.

7. Serve with keto bread!

Nutrition:

Calories 368,

Fat 3,

Fiber 4,

Carbs 53.34,

Protein 7

Prawn Stew

Preparation time: 15 minutes

Cooking time: 1 hour

Servings: 4

Ingredients:

- 10 oz. prawns, peeled

- 1 onion, sliced

- 4 oz. Parmesan, grated

- 1 garlic clove, peeled

- 1 teaspoon salt

- ½ cup almond milk

- 1 teaspoon butter

- 1 teaspoon chili flakes

Directions:

1. Place the peeled prawns, sliced onion, garlic clove, salt, almond milk, butter, and chili flakes into the slow cooker.

2. Close the lid and cook the stew for 1 hour on High.

3. Transfer the cooked stew into serving bowls and sprinkle with the grated cheese.

4. Serve it!

Nutrition:

Calories 278,

Fat 7.5,

Fiber 2,

Carbs 36.74,

Protein 10

Pork-Jalapeno Bowl

Preparation time: 15 minutes

Cooking time: 3 hours

Servings: 4

Ingredients:

- 2 jalapeno peppers, chopped

- 9 oz. pork chops

- 1 onion, grated

- ½ cup water

- 1 teaspoon butter

- ½ teaspoon chili flakes

- 1 teaspoon ground black pepper

Directions:

1. Sprinkle the pork chops with the chili flakes and ground black pepper.

2. Place the pork chops in the slow cooker.

3. Add water, grated onion, and butter,

4. Add the jalapeno peppers and close the lid.

5. Cook the meal for 3 hours on High.

6. Stir the cooked meal and transfer it to serving bowls.

7. Serve it!

Nutrition:

Calories 148,

Fat 7.5,

Fiber 2,

Carbs 36.74,

Protein 10

Chicken Marsala

Preparation time: 15 minutes

Cooking time: 7 hours

Servings: 4

Ingredients:

- 1-pound chicken breast, skinless, boneless

- 2 oz. white mushrooms, chopped

- 1 Oz Marsala cooking wine

- 1 teaspoon garlic powder

- 3 tablespoons butter

- 1 teaspoon salt

- 1 teaspoon ground black pepper

Directions:

1. Chop the chicken breast roughly and sprinkle it with the garlic powder, salt, and ground black pepper.

2. Stir the chicken and transfer it to the slow cooker.

3. Add butter, Marsala cooking wine, mushrooms, and close the lid.

4. Cook chicken Marsala for 7 hours on Low.

5. Stir the cooked meal gently.

6. Serve it in serving bowls.

7. Enjoy!

Nutrition:

Calories 248,

Fat 7.5,

Fiber 2,

Carbs 36.74,

Protein 10

Chickpeas Soup

Preparation time: 10 minutes

Cooking time: 4 hours

Servings: 6

Ingredients:

- 30 ounces canned chickpeas, drained

- 2 tablespoons mild curry powder

- 1 cup lentils, dry

- 1 sweet potato, cubed

- 15 ounces canned coconut milk

- 1 teaspoon ginger powder

- 1 teaspoon turmeric, ground

- A pinch of salt

- 6 cups veggie stock

- Black pepper to the taste

Directions:

1. Put chickpeas in your slow cooker.

2. Add lentils, sweet potato cubes, curry powder, ginger, turmeric, salt, pepper and stock.

3. Stir and then mix with coconut milk.

4. Stir again, cover and cook on High for 4 hours.

5. Ladle chickpeas soup into bowls and serve.

6. Enjoy!

Nutrition:

Calories: 302g,

Fat: 22g,

Carbs: 5g,

Protein: 34g,

Hot and Delicious Soup

Preparation time: 10 minutes

Cooking time: 8 hours

Servings: 4

Ingredients:

- 8 ounces canned bamboo shoots, drained and chopped
- 10 ounces mushrooms, sliced
- 8 shiitake mushrooms, sliced
- 4 garlic cloves, minced
- 2 tablespoons ginger, grated
- 15 ounces extra firm tofu, pressed and cubed
- 2 tablespoons vegan bouillon
- 4 cups water
- 1 teaspoon sesame oil
- 2 tablespoons coconut aminos
- 1 teaspoon chili paste
- 1 and ½ cups peas
- 2 tablespoons rice wine vinegar

Directions:

1. Put the water in your slow cooker.

2. Add bamboo shoot, mushrooms, shiitake mushrooms, garlic, 1 tablespoon ginger, tofu, vegan bouillon, oil, aminos, chili paste, peas and vinegar.

3. Stir, cover and cook on Low for 8 hours.

4. Add the rest of the ginger, stir soup again, ladle into bowls and serve right away.

5. Enjoy!

Nutrition:

Calories: 102g,

Fat: 22g,

Carbs: 5g,

Protein: 34g,

Delicious Eggplant Salad

Preparation time: 10 minutes

Cooking time: 8 hours

Servings: 4

Ingredients:

- 1 big eggplant, cut into quarters and then sliced
- 25 ounces canned plum tomatoes
- 2 red bell peppers, chopped
- 1 red onion, sliced
- 2 teaspoons cumin, ground
- A pinch of sea salt
- Black pepper to the taste
- 1 teaspoon smoked paprika
- Juice of 1 lemon

Directions:

1. In your slow cooker, mix eggplant pieces with tomatoes, bell peppers, onion, cumin, salt, pepper, paprika and lemon juice, stir, cover and cook on Low for 8 hours.

2. Stir again, divide into bowls and serve cold.

3. Enjoy!

Nutrition:

Calories: 302g,

Fat: 22g,

Carbs: 5g,

Protein: 34g,

Tasty Black Beans Soup

Preparation time: 10 minutes

Cooking time: 6 hours

Servings: 6

Ingredients:

- 4 cups veggie stock

- 1 pound black beans, soaked overnight and drained

- 1 yellow onion, chopped

- 2 jalapenos, chopped

- 1 red bell pepper, chopped

- 1 cup tomatoes, chopped

- 4 garlic cloves, minced

- 1 tablespoon chili powder

- Black pepper to the taste

- 2 teaspoons cumin, ground

- A pinch of sea salt

- ½ teaspoon cayenne pepper

- 1 avocado, pitted, peeled and chopped

- ½ teaspoon sweet paprika

Directions:

1. Put the stock in your slow cooker.

2. Add beans, onion, jalapenos, bell pepper, tomatoes, garlic, chili powder, black pepper, salt, cumin, cayenne and paprika.

3. Stir, cover and cook on Low for 6 hours.

4. Blend soup using an immersion blender, ladle into bowls and serve with chopped avocado on top.

5. Enjoy!

Nutrition:

Calories: 202g,

Fat: 22g,

Carbs: 5g,

Protein: 34g,

Rich Sweet Potato Soup

Preparation time: 10 minutes

Cooking time: 8 hours

Servings: 5

Ingredients:

- 5 cups veggie stock

- 2 celery stalks, chopped

- 3 sweet potatoes, chopped

- 1 cup yellow onion, chopped

- 2 garlic cloves, minced

- 1 cup rice milk

- 1 teaspoon tarragon, dried

- 2 cups baby spinach

- 8 tablespoons almonds, sliced

- A pinch of salt

- Black pepper to the taste

Directions:

1. Put the stock in your slow cooker.

2. Add celery, potatoes, onion, garlic, salt, pepper and tarragon.

3. Stir, cover and cook on Low for 8 hours.

4. Add rice milk and blend using an immersion blender.

5. Add almonds and spinach, stir, cover and leave aside for 20 minutes.

6. Ladle into bowls and serve.

7. Enjoy!

Nutrition:

Calories: 302g,

Fat: 22g,

Carbs: 5g,

Protein: 34g,

Pumpkin Chili

Preparation time: 10 minutes

Cooking time: 8 hours

Servings: 6

Ingredients:

- 1 cup pumpkin, pureed
- 45 ounces canned black beans, drained
- 30 ounces canned tomatoes, chopped
- 1 yellow bell pepper, chopped
- 1 yellow onion, chopped
- ¼ teaspoon nutmeg, ground
- 1 teaspoon cinnamon powder
- 1 tablespoon chili powder
- 1 teaspoon cumin, ground
- 1/8 teaspoon cloves, ground
- A pinch of sea salt
- Black pepper to the taste

Directions:

1. Put pumpkin puree in your slow cooker.

2. Add black beans, tomatoes, onion, bell pepper, cumin, nutmeg, cinnamon, chili powder, cloves, salt and pepper, stir, cover and cook on Low for 8 hours.

3. Stir your chili again, divide into bowls and serve.

4. Enjoy!

Nutrition:

Calories: 242g,

Fat: 22g,

Carbs: 5g,

Protein: 34g,

CPSIA information can be obtained
at www.ICGtesting.com
Printed in the USA
BVHW051509080321
601999BV00001BB/36